JONES of COLORADO

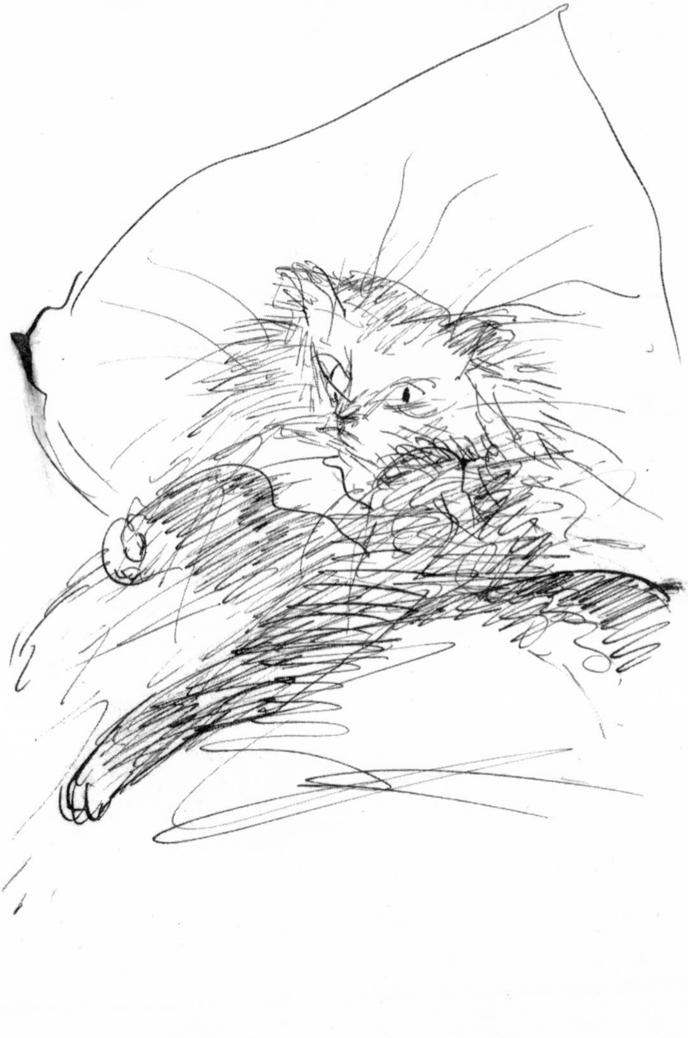

EBURY PRESS
LONDON

Entrance to Owl Farm   Woody

JONES of COLORADO

Home of JONES. Ralph STEADman

TO LAILA NABULSI
Beauty to the beasts

First published in 1995

1 3 5 7 9 10 8 6 4 2

First published in the United Kingdom in 1995 by Ebury
Press, Random House, 20 Vauxhall Bridge Road, London,
SW1V 2SA

Random House Australia (Pty) Limited
20 Alfred Street, Milsons Point, Sydney,
New South Wales 2061, Australia

Random House New Zealand Limited
18 Poland Road, Glenfield,
Auckland 10, New Zealand

Random House South Africa (Pty) Limited
PO Box 337, Bergvlei, South Africa

Random House UK Limited Reg. No. 954009

A CIP catalogue record for this book is available from the
British Library.

Design: Ian Craig
Copy Editor: Pascal Cariss

ISBN 0 09 180945 2

Printed and bound in Great Britain by Butler & Tanner,
Frome, England

Jones wants to come in .

If I had really wanted to do a book about cats, I would have done it years ago. But Jones is dead, and if ever a cat should be remembered, it's Jones. I only met him the once, for just two weeks, but in that time he left a deep impression.

I was staying in Woody Creek, Colorado, as a guest of the writer Hunter S. Thompson, my collaborator on many maverick assignments.

With his lovely girlfriend, Laila Nabulsi, we were trying to lash together a book we had found ourselves the victims of, called The Curse of Lono, and the curse was fast overtaking our efforts. But that's what acts of creation are all about; like childbirth, there are spasms of pain, periods of inertia, contractions - and then, if you're lucky, some kind of offspring, with its father's eyes and a mother's smile.

Hunter had kept other animals over the years, chosen as one does any pet, impulsively and from what's available at the time. But Jones chose Hunter, or at least Hunter's house. It suited his purpose right down to the tip of his bushy tail.

Jones on The Carpet

Pretty Jones.

The only creatures in the house likely to cause Jones any competition for affection were Hunter's peacocks, but they were too bizarre to confront with a challenge. Jones just let them be, like the smart cat he was. Anyway, there were five of them, and even one is too many if you want to wring its bloody neck.

Jones and Hunter's
Peacock S.

Jones weighs up a Peacock

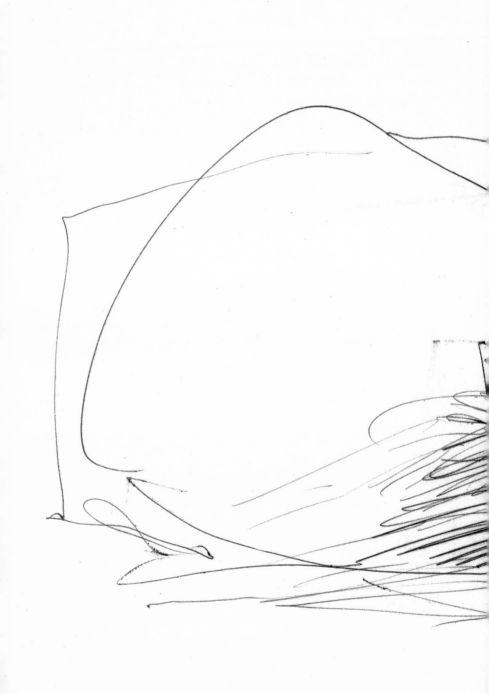

So Jones stayed and, by the looks of things when I turned up, very much on his own terms. He and his master shared a deep and guarded respect, a kind of mutual recognition of each other's stealth in matters of survival.

It was Laila who fed the two of them, and both in their strange ways were treated like pets who required special treatment. Both made demands and were locked into worlds reserved for selfish gods. Nobody could complain about that since terms of existence, wherever gods find themselves, are absolute. And in most circumstances I accept the general pattern of daily life, no matter how weird, as normal. Otherwise, how do you survive?

Jones
on his
pedestal.

Jones in luck.

Jones being lifted.

Perhaps only a cat would try something unaccountable and against the grain, while purring softly, arching the back, and rubbing itself enticingly against you. That's why they get away with it.

Jones in torment

Cats have been known to smother a baby in a cot out of pure love of luxury and ecstatic warmth, then curl themselves around a leg for nothing more than praise. They are the personification of evil yet they can do no wrong. They exist, are utterly themselves, and, no matter how fierce the storm raging around them, find the warmest place to be.

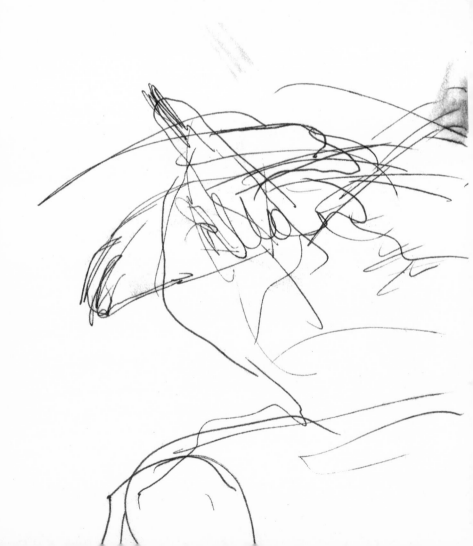

Jones
Cares.

Jones turns
a cold
shoulder.

It took me two days to feel the full weight of his authority, and when I did, I decided to buy a handsome sketchbook from a store in Aspen and try to catch something of his arch presence. God knows, I'm not much of an animal person - at home I try to cope with three sheep and one tiny rabbit, and so far I have three bags of wool and a ton of rabbit shit.

2-second Jones.

One-way Jones

Emotions depend on your frame of mind at a particular time. Even a cathedral is simply a bunch of big stones if you are feeling bloody minded. Maybe Jones filled an empty space majestically at the right moment. He commanded by veneration like the leader of a new cult.

Jones
plays
God.

I am trying to remember when I first caught a particularly virulent dose of Jones's clawed charm... His fur swelled from his cheeks like a display of carnival fireworks, but he wasn't smiling at me, he was drawing from within himself the unbearable pleasures of his own world. His acknowledgement was nothing more than a passing reflection of my existence, a sounding board; a possible source of some diversion he had not yet thought of. He had no other use for me.

A touch of Jones.

What the hell! The world needs creatures like Jones to remind us that, if we are honest, we are selfish too. If you think you are a saint, try to prove it, but you will not be loved.

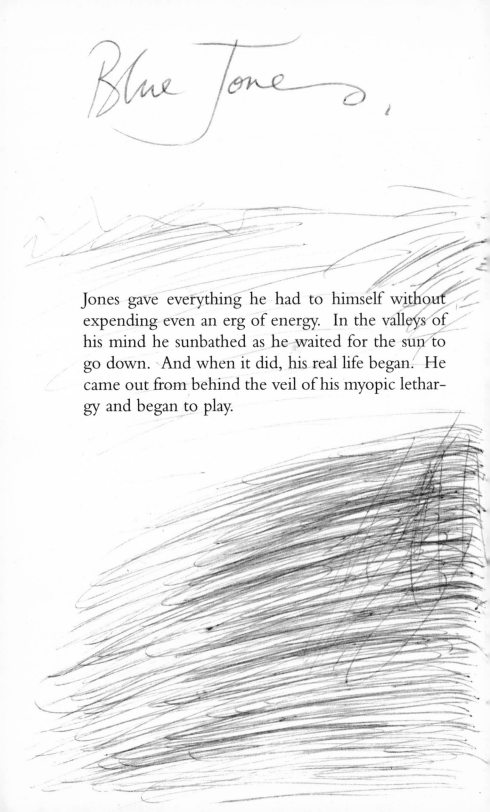

Jones gave everything he had to himself without expending even an erg of energy. In the valleys of his mind he sunbathed as he waited for the sun to go down. And when it did, his real life began. He came out from behind the veil of his myopic lethargy and began to play.

Jones watches the
sun go down

Some cats play like kittens. They display the boundless energy of the newborn. They are coy and self-conscious, but eager to engage in confrontation. They fall on their backs and tumble like autumn leaves. Eyes bright with anticipation, jaws wide open, they show and contemplate the vulnerable underbelly. Then suddenly they are up and at you with the instincts of a lion but hardly the strength of a baby.

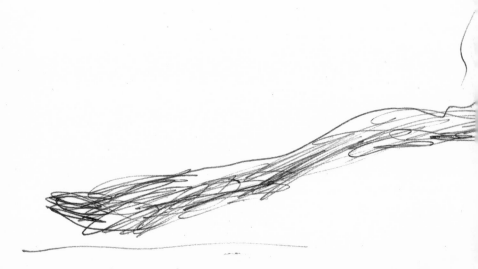

Jones growls softly.

Jones guarding
his territory

Jones did none of that. He played like a bored Roman emperor tolerating the entertainment offered by gladiators and Christians. He had seen it all before.

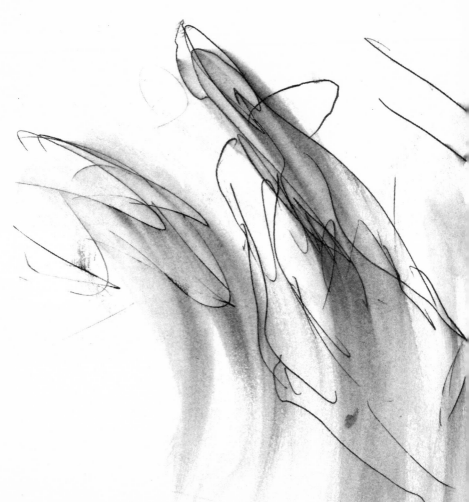

Jones allowed you to make the first move and watched languidly as you did so. He would lie like an eagle's wing across a couch, and the last thing in his mind was playing, least of all with someone other than himself, and certainly not with a stranger.

Foolishly, you ruffle the fur on his exposed stomach; anybody would, it is always so soft and inviting. We have common ways of saying 'No' to an advance, but a cat has to use a nameless guile to ward off the unwanted playful lunge.

Jones knew what to do at once. A savage paw on the back of my hand was all I needed to encourage me to do something else. I learned when it was wrong to cross Jones. He would not tolerate mindless stupidity, which is probably why Hunter and he understood each other so well.

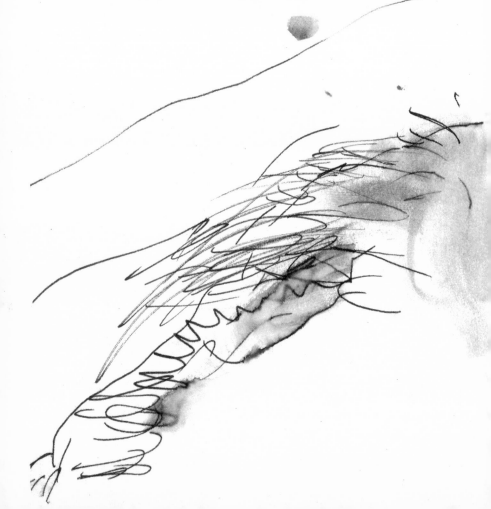

He could, however, adopt a pathetic and pleading demeanour when he wanted something that only you could do for him, such as open the door on to the rolling outdoors of his domain. Yet, after a few seconds, if his patience had been stretched by your hesitation, he would growl gently for immediate action. Those were the very times when his appeal was irresistible, causing a great surge of love and admiration to charge my creative spring.

I needed to capture some of these moments, and the best way I know is with a few direct lines, straight from the eye through the mind to the hand. The result on paper can be fiendishly perceptive or hopelessly inaccurate, but it is always an intriguing and playful possibility.

Jane
wants to go
OUT.

Tones in Trafalgar Square.

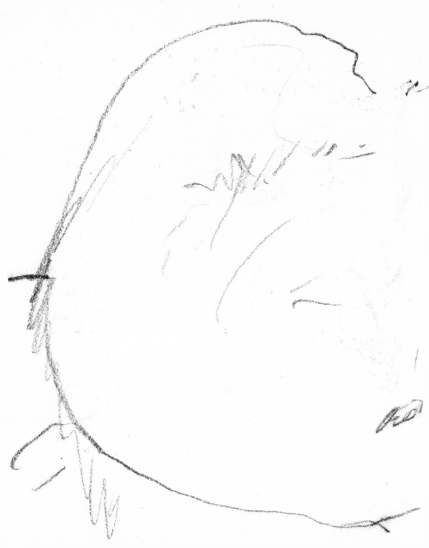

Drawing often has this power, which may account for the intense interest shown when anyone makes an impression on paper. No matter how pedestrian the result, we feel that something mysterious and rare has happened within a private world, and we are privileged to witness it in this vague and doubtful revelation.

In my drawings, Jones decided the style and I went along with it, being the weaker of the two parties. Jones had a manner which engaged many people. His domestic remoteness was a spur rather than a hindrance to natural affinity. He found his place and knew it. He coveted nothing but his own comfort, and lacked only a god's control over his own fate.

My drawings are a scrambled response – the grab-
bing of a sketchpad, the frantic search for the pen
or chalk at the knife-edge moment when Jones had
come to rest in an attitude of high condescension,
the outward manifestation of a flitting mood or of
his brooding inner spirit. They are nearly cartoons,
but essentially my serious attempt to capture the
finer artistry of Jones's posture, and often merely a
wisp of memory registered by the eye as he floated
through my gaze. Our close detachment came
about because we were often the only ones awake.
Since Hunter's habits and activities are nocturnal,
the rest of the household slept the early part of the
day away.

Tones Venturing
sonle more

Jones in the throes of uncertainty.

On many nights I struggled to stay up so we could work together, but I still needed to go to bed during the dark hours. I find it impossible to sleep without guilt when the day has come. Perhaps my Welsh mining ancestry on my mother's side is responsible for this. Honest work is a daily activity which begins with the coming of light. The night is for sleeping and private acts of creation.

So I stalked the house all day between fitful bursts
of drawing for our book, seemingly alone with the
muted sounds of peacocks on the balcony outside,
the electric hum of the stereo equipment and the

hiccuping fridge, the raucous burst of an occasional phone-call feeding the answering machine, and silence enough to detect the purring of Jones as he wallowed through the trough of the day ...

The early autumn colours of change gently tinted the old log cabin ambience and a cooler sun broke into the house like blocks of glowing ice, illuminating a corner and shedding a reflected light over the couch where Jones lay haloed – and I watched him. Maybe he would look in my direction through a haze of half closed shimmering eyelash eyes with an unerring appreciation of his own smug self-satisfaction.

Then, as though a meandering thought of some previous engagement pricked his bubble mind like a wasp sting, with swift stealth he was seated by the door, throwing back at me his imploring look before it froze into a stony glare and gained my dutiful response. Thy will be done.

And so it was.

'Sour
Puss!
Jones.

In those two weeks, odd friends, famous, infamous, pleasant and obscure came and went, stayed and dabbled, made arrangements, laughed and ate, and slept on sofas. Jones treated everyone with similar detente. Each was a moving thing to tease his whim with respect and worship at the alter he had made his own. None meant more than that, for somewhere in his mysterious past, there gnawed a faceless memory; perhaps a thoughtless indiscretion when he had given all his love and trust to such a moving thing as those around him now. Maybe it was a tragic disappointment and he had learned, as much by instinct as by guile, that where he stood was all he could expect, and thereby laid his claim.

Jones relaxing.

Then I, like all the rest, left. For all Jones cared we might never have met. I was just another passing entertainment.

Later, Laila came to visit me in England. "How's Jones?" I said.

"Jones is dead," she told me, "and that's how I heard it. Just like that." She had rung Hunter and she too had asked, "How's Jones." He struggled to tell her

Jones in
my bed,

gently, but hesitant explanations merely triggered the desire to get it over with, and the truth tumbled out abruptly. "He's dead. JONES IS DEAD!"

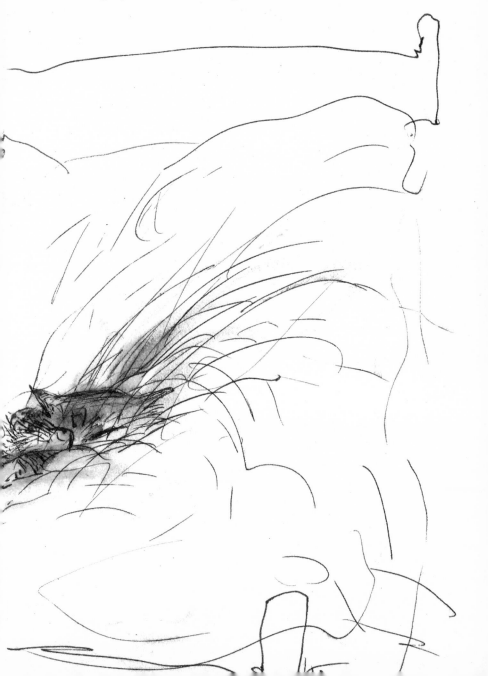

Laila told me how he died, but I forget and maybe I don't really want to know. Perhaps I will ask Hunter when I next see him...

Jones on the other side.